This book belongs to

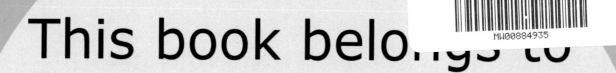

_____

My Chinese name is

_____

Hi, I'm Java. Let's start learning.

Cantonese: jat1
Mandarin: yī

One

Draw one apple

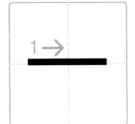  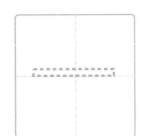 

   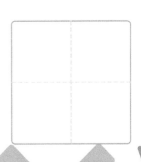

Cantonese: ji6
Mandarin: èr

二
Two

Date : _____

Circle two strawberries

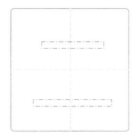

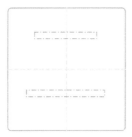

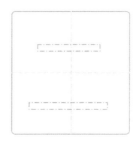
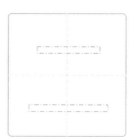

Cantonese: saam1
Mandarin: sān

三

Three

Color three birds

 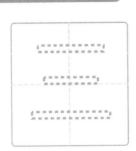 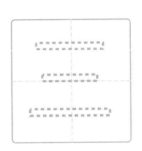 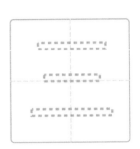

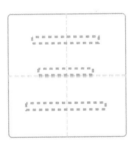 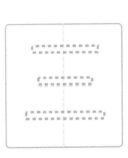 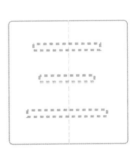 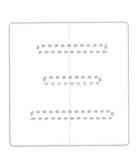

 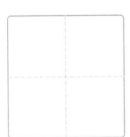  

Date : _____

Cantonese: sei3
Mandarin: sì

四
Four

Name four of your favorite food

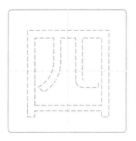 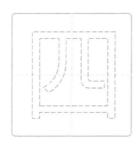 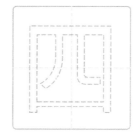 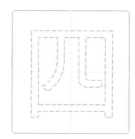

五
Cantonese: ng5
Mandarin: wǔ
Five

Color the number 5

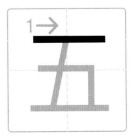 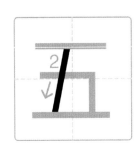 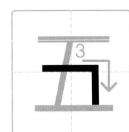 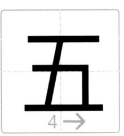

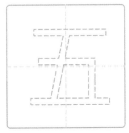 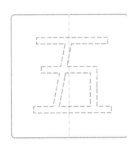 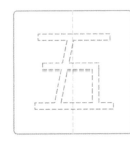 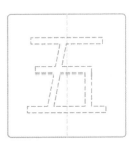

六
Cantonese: luk6
Mandarin: liù

Six

Color 6 bananas

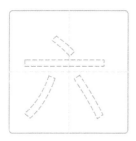 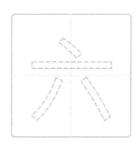  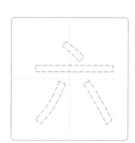

   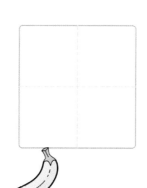

Cantonese: cat1
Mandarin: qī

七

Seven

Color the rainbow

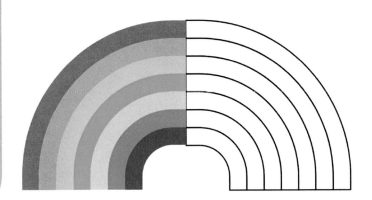

 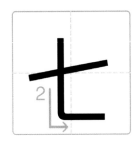 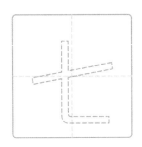 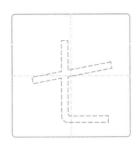

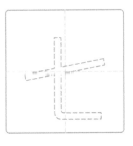 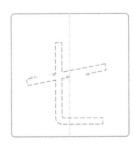 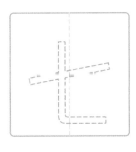 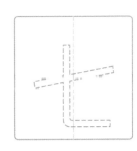

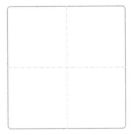   

Cantonese: baat3
Mandarin: bā

八

Eight

Color the octopus

 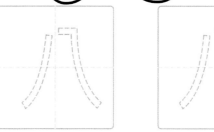

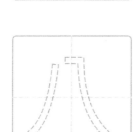  

8   8   8   8   8   8   8   8

Cantonese: gau2
Mandarin: jiǔ

九
Nine

Color 9 fish

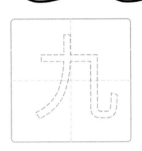
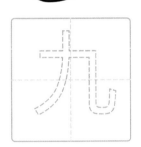

Cantonese: sap6
Mandarin: shí

十

Ten

Color the bees

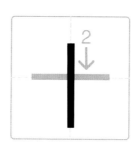

1→ 2↓

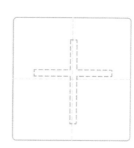

Cantonese: daai6
Mandarin: dà

大
Big

Color the big flowers

  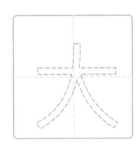 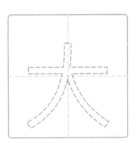

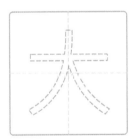 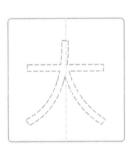 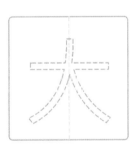 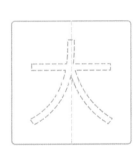

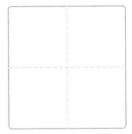   

小

Cantonese: siu2
Mandarin: xiǎo

Small

Color the small flowers

  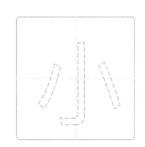 

Cantonese: soeng5
Mandarin: shàng

上
Up

Which one is pointing up?

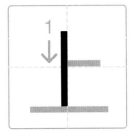
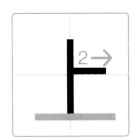
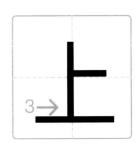
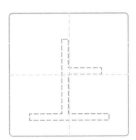

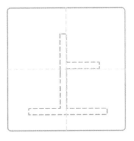
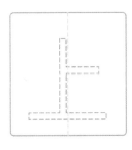
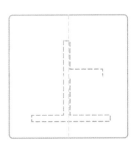
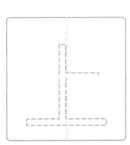

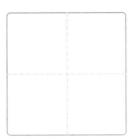

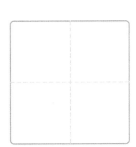

下
Cantonese: haa6
Mandarin: xià
Down

Which one is pointing down?

 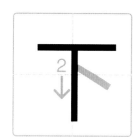  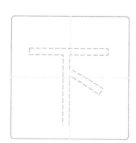

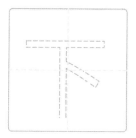 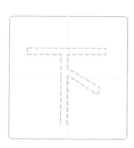  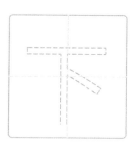

Cantonese: zo2
Mandarin: zuǒ

左
Left

Which one is pointing left?

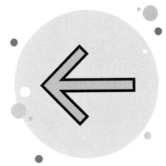 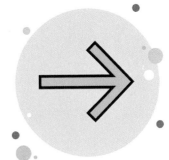

   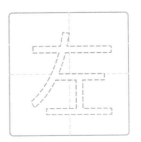

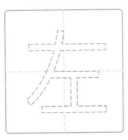 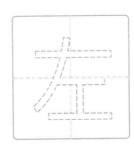 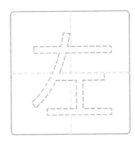 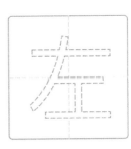

右
Cantonese: jau6
Mandarin: yòu
Right

Which one is pointing right?

   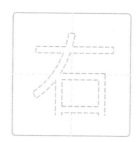

   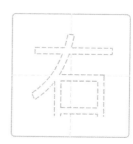

Do you remember how to write 1 to 10 in Chinese? Let's practice.

Java

One  1

Six  6

Two  2

Seven  7

Three  3

Eight  8

Four  4

Nine  9

Five  5

Ten  10

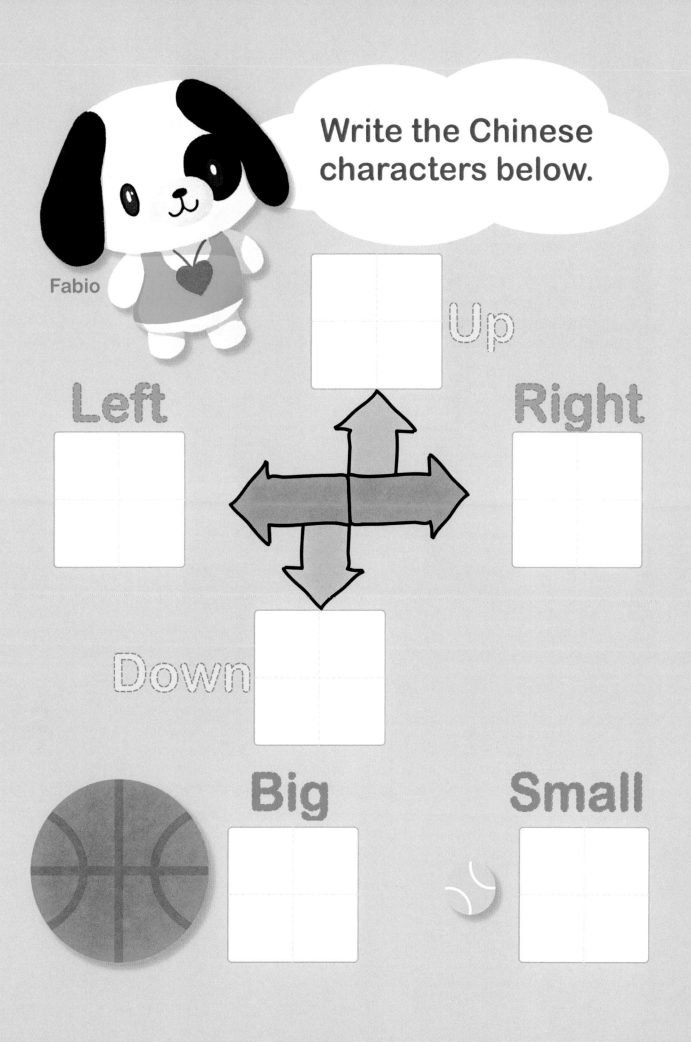

Date : _____

男
Boy

Cantonese: naam4
Mandarin: nán

Draw a boy

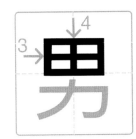

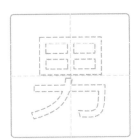

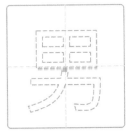
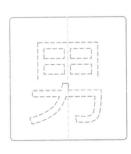

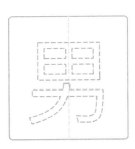

Date : _____

Draw a girl

Cantonese: neoi5
Mandarin: nǚ

女
Girl

   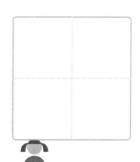

Date : _____

Cantonese: jan4
Mandarin: rén

人
Person

Draw your favorite person

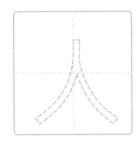
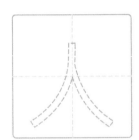

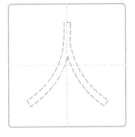
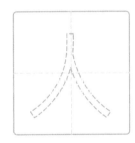
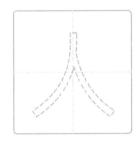
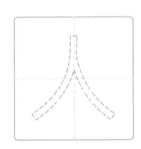

耳
Cantonese: ji5
Mandarin: ěr

Ear

Draw the bunny ears

 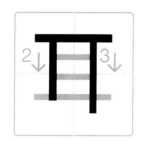  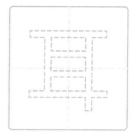

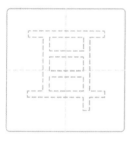  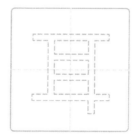 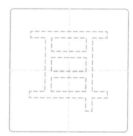

Date : _____

Cantonese: hau2
Mandarin: kǒu

Mouth

Circle the mouth

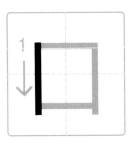
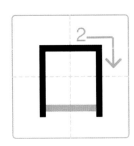
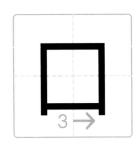
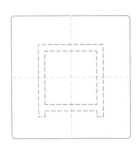

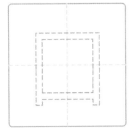
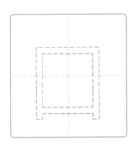
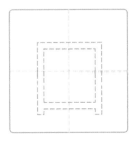
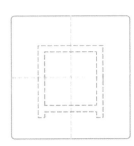

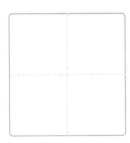

Cantonese: sau2
Mandarin: shǒu

手
Hand

Draw your hand

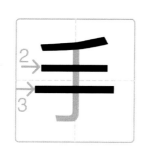

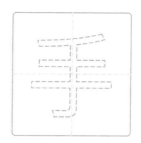

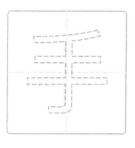
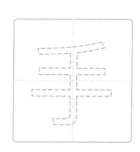

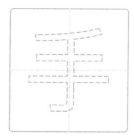

Date : _____

Cantonese: sam1
Mandarin: xīn

心 Heart

Color the hearts

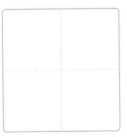  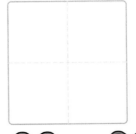 

Pink Pink

Match the words and pictures. Then write the Chinese characters.

Person •

Ear •

Mouth •

Hand •

Heart •

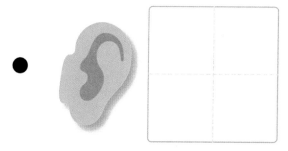

山

Cantonese: saan1
Mandarin: shān

Mountain

Color the mountains

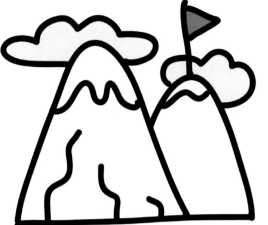

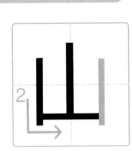 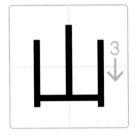 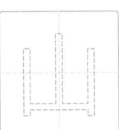 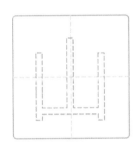

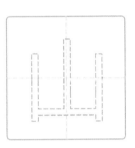 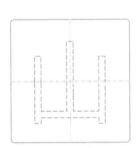  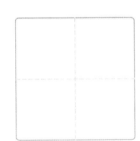

Date : _____

Cantonese: seoi2
Mandarin: shuǐ

水
Water

Color the water drops

Cantonese: tou2
Mandarin: tǔ

土

Soil

Color the soil

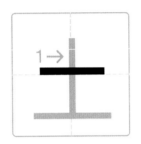

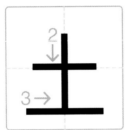

Cantonese: fo2
Mandarin: huǒ

火
Fire

Color the fire

  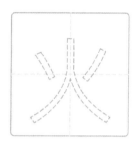 

 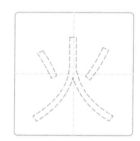 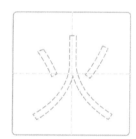 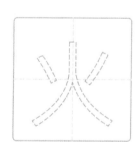

Cantonese: muk6
Mandarin: mù

木
Wood

Color the wood

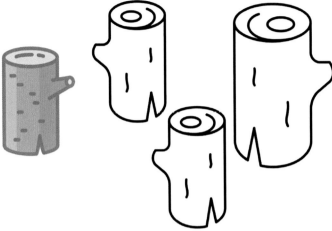

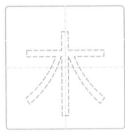

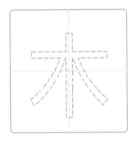
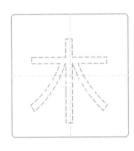
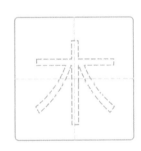
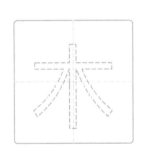

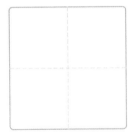

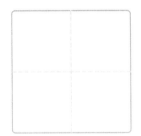

天
Cantonese: tin1
Mandarin: tiān
Sky

Circle what you can find in the sky

  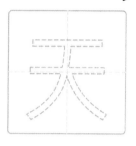 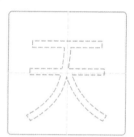

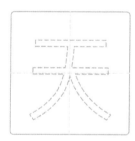 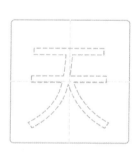 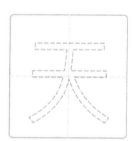 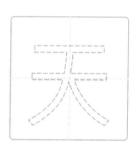

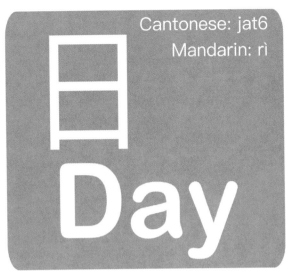

Cantonese: jat6
Mandarin: rì

日
Day

Color the sun

Date : _____

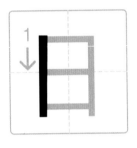
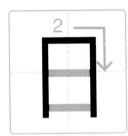

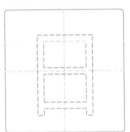

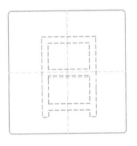
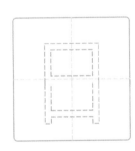

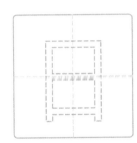

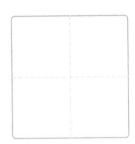

月
Cantonese: jyut6
Mandarin: yuè

Moon

Color the moon

   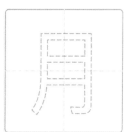

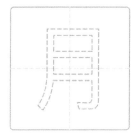 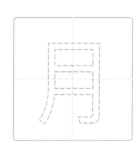 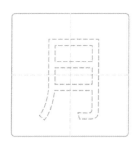 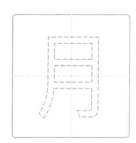

  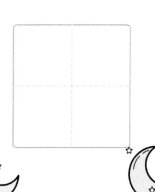 

Date : _____

早

Cantonese: zou2
Mandarin: zǎo

Morning

Color
Fabio

Good
morning!

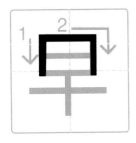 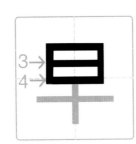  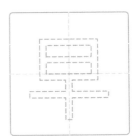

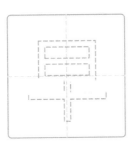 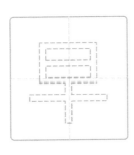 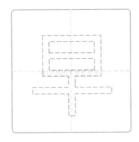 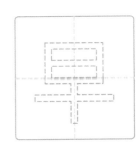

午

Cantonese: ng5
Mandarin: wŭ

Afternoon

Color
Pink Pink

Good
afternoon!

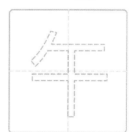
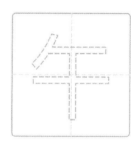

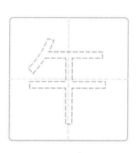
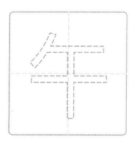
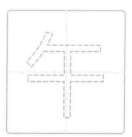

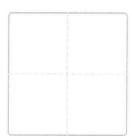
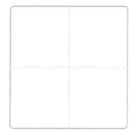

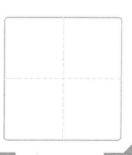

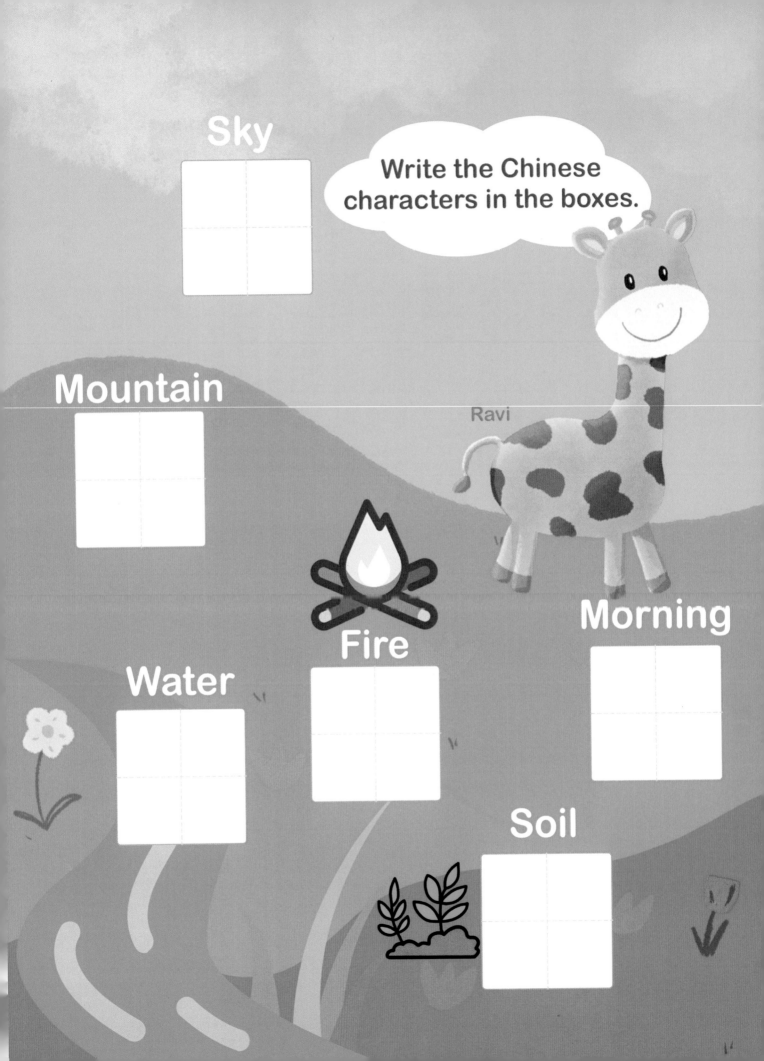

Made in the USA
Las Vegas, NV
30 November 2024